First World War
and Army of Occupation
War Diary
France, Belgium and Germany

21 DIVISION
Headquarters, Branches and Services
Royal Army Veterinary Corps
Assistant Director Veterinary Services
9 September 1915 - 31 March 1919

WO95/2140/3

The Naval & Military Press Ltd
www.nmarchive.com
Published in association with The National Archives

Published by

The Naval & Military Press Ltd

Unit 10 Ridgewood Industrial Park,

Uckfield, East Sussex,

TN22 5QE England

Tel: +44 (0) 1825 749494

www.naval-military-press.com

www.nmarchive.com

This diary has been reprinted in facsimile from the original. Any imperfections are inevitably reproduced and the quality may fall short of modern type and cartographic standards.

Contents

Document type	Place/Title	Date From	Date To
Heading	WO95/2140/3		
Heading	21st Division Asst Dir. Vety Services Sep 1915-Mar 1919		
Heading	H.Q. 21st Div: A.D.V.S. Vol I Sept To Oct 15		
War Diary	Havre	09/09/1915	09/09/1915
War Diary	St Omer	10/09/1915	10/09/1915
War Diary	Watten	11/09/1915	20/09/1915
War Diary	Aguin Shem	21/09/1915	22/09/1915
War Diary	Norrent Fontes	22/09/1915	22/09/1915
War Diary	Ferfey	23/09/1915	24/09/1915
War Diary	Noeux Les Mines	25/09/1915	25/09/1915
War Diary	Philosophe	25/09/1915	29/09/1915
War Diary	Bethune	30/09/1915	30/09/1915
War Diary	Liettres	30/09/1915	01/10/1915
War Diary	Mor Becque	01/10/1915	02/10/1915
War Diary	Hondeghem	02/10/1915	06/10/1915
War Diary	Merris	06/10/1915	30/10/1915
Heading	H.Q. 21st Div. A.D.V.S. Vol 2 Nov. 15		
War Diary	Merris	01/11/1915	12/11/1915
War Diary	Armentieres	13/11/1915	30/11/1915
Heading	A.D.V.S. 21st Div: Vol: 3		
War Diary	Armentieres	01/12/1915	30/12/1915
Heading	A.D.V.S. 21st Div: Vol 4		
War Diary	Armentieres	01/01/1916	25/01/1916
Heading	A.D.V.S. 21st Div: Vol. 5		
War Diary	Armentieres	04/02/1916	29/02/1916
Heading	ADVS 21st Div Vol 6		
War Diary	Armentieres	01/03/1916	31/03/1916
War Diary	Ribemont	01/04/1916	30/06/1916
War Diary	Ville	01/07/1916	04/07/1916
War Diary	Belloy Sur Somme	05/07/1916	07/07/1916
War Diary	Ribemont	10/07/1916	12/07/1916
War Diary	Meault	14/07/1916	20/07/1916
War Diary	Le Cauroy	22/07/1916	29/07/1916
War Diary	Duisans	30/07/1916	05/09/1916
War Diary	Le Cauroy	06/09/1916	30/09/1916
War Diary	Fricourt	01/10/1916	01/10/1916
War Diary	Buire	02/10/1916	02/10/1916
War Diary	Ailly Le Haut Clocher	03/10/1916	07/10/1916
War Diary	Noeux Les Mines	08/10/1916	11/10/1916
War Diary	Sailly Les Bourse	12/10/1916	22/11/1916
Miscellaneous	A.G's Office, Base.	18/01/1917	18/01/1917
War Diary	Sailly Les Bourse	02/12/1916	31/12/1916
Miscellaneous	A.G.'s Office, Base.	11/03/1917	11/03/1917
War Diary	Labeuvriere	01/01/1917	28/01/1917
War Diary	Wormhout	03/02/1917	15/02/1917
War Diary	Sailly-Labourse	01/03/1917	11/03/1917
War Diary	Lvcheeux	12/03/1917	29/03/1917
War Diary	Bavincourt	29/03/1917	04/04/1917
War Diary	Adinfer	05/04/1917	26/04/1917

War Diary	Hamelincourt	27/04/1917	12/05/1917
War Diary	Adinfer Wood	13/05/1917	31/05/1917
War Diary	Hamelincourt	01/06/1917	30/06/1917
War Diary	Moyenville	01/07/1917	30/08/1917
War Diary	Duisans	27/08/1917	16/09/1917
War Diary	Caestre	16/09/1917	23/09/1917
War Diary	Meteren	23/09/1917	29/09/1917
War Diary	Scottish Wood	29/09/1917	08/10/1917
War Diary	Blaringhem	08/10/1917	20/10/1917
War Diary	Zevecoten	20/10/1917	23/10/1917
War Diary	Chateau Segard	23/10/1917	16/11/1917
War Diary	Veux Berquin	16/11/1917	16/11/1917
War Diary	Barlin	18/11/1917	18/11/1917
War Diary	Victory Camp	22/11/1917	22/11/1917
War Diary	Villers Chatel	22/11/1917	22/11/1917
War Diary	Tincourt	01/12/1917	24/12/1917
War Diary	Longavesnes	24/12/1917	02/02/1918
War Diary	Havt Allaines	03/02/1918	28/02/1918
War Diary	Longavesnes	01/03/1918	21/03/1918
War Diary	Templeux-La-Fosse	22/03/1918	29/03/1918
Heading	D.A.G. 3rd Echelon Base		
War Diary	Dranoutre	01/04/1918	10/04/1918
War Diary	Chateau Segard	11/04/1918	11/04/1918
War Diary	Hoograaf	17/04/1918	17/04/1918
War Diary	Poperinghe G 16 a 5.2 Sheet 28	19/04/1918	30/04/1918
War Diary	L.14.a.20	01/05/1918	01/05/1918
War Diary	Rubrouck	02/05/1918	04/05/1918
War Diary	Romigny	05/05/1918	15/05/1918
War Diary	Chalons Les-Vergeur	15/05/1918	27/05/1918
War Diary	Prouilly	28/05/1918	28/05/1918
War Diary	Chaltrait	31/05/1918	09/06/1918
War Diary	La Node	10/06/1918	10/06/1918
War Diary	Disemont	15/06/1918	19/06/1918
War Diary	Gamaches	22/06/1918	30/06/1918
War Diary	Beauquesne	01/07/1918	22/07/1918
War Diary	Raincheval	25/07/1918	31/08/1918
War Diary	Mailly Maillet	01/09/1918	01/09/1918
War Diary	Le Sars	06/09/1918	06/09/1918
War Diary	Les Boeufs	07/09/1918	28/09/1918
Heading	War Diary D.A.D.V.S. 21st Division October 1st-31st 1918		
War Diary	Le Mesnil	01/10/1918	01/10/1918
War Diary	Equancourt	06/10/1918	08/10/1918
War Diary	Revelon Farm	09/10/1918	09/10/1918
War Diary	Bantouzelle	10/10/1918	10/10/1918
War Diary	Warlincourt	11/10/1918	15/10/1918
War Diary	Inchy	22/10/1918	22/10/1918
War Diary	Neuvilly	25/10/1918	31/10/1918
Heading	War Diary of D.A.D.V.S. 21st Division. From 1st November 1918 To 30th November 1918 Vol 39		
War Diary	Neuvilly	01/11/1918	02/11/1918
War Diary	??	04/11/1918	06/11/1918
War Diary	Berlemont	11/11/1918	30/11/1918
Heading	War Diary of D.A.D.V.S. 21st Division. From 1st December 1918 To 31st December 1918 Vol 40		
War Diary	Aulnoye	01/12/1918	16/12/1918

War Diary	Molliens-Vidame	16/12/1918	29/12/1918
War Diary	Ailly-Sur-Somme	29/12/1918	31/12/1918
Heading	War Diary of D.A.D.V.S. 21st Division. From 1st January 1919 To 31st January 1919 Vol 41		
War Diary	Ailly-Sur-Somme	01/01/1919	28/01/1919
Heading	War Diary of D.A.D.V.S. 21st Division. From 1st February 1919 To 28th February 1919 Vol 42		
War Diary	Ailly Sur Somme	03/02/1919	29/03/1919
War Diary	Picquigny	29/03/1919	31/03/1919

21ST DIVISION

ASST DIR.VETY SERVICES

SEP 1915 - MAR 1919

121
7517

H.Q. 21st Div: A.D.V.S.

Vol I

Sept & Oct. 15

Q

Ano

Instructions regarding War Diaries and Intelligence Summaries are contained in F. S. Regs., Part II. and the Staff Manual respectively. Title Pages will be prepared in manuscript.

WAR DIARY

~~or~~

~~INTELLIGENCE SUMMARY~~

(Erase heading not required.)

A.D.V.S
21 Div

Army Form C. 2118

Place	Date	Hour	Summary of Events and Information	Remarks and references to Appendices
HAVRE	Sept 9th	7am	Arrived in France i/c HQ & MMP Horses	
"	"	10pm	Entrained	
ST OMER	10th	5pm	Dis-Entrained and marched to WATTEN	
WATTEN	11th-20th	–	Inspecting MVS & animals of the Division..	
"	20th	9pm	Marched out	
AGUINGHEM	21st	4am	Arrived –	
"	22nd	8pm	Marched out	
[illegible]RRENT FONTES	"	3am	Arrived. Inspected Remounts LILLIERS Station in afternoon. & Horse S.D.H.	
"	"	7pm	Marched out	
FERFEY	23rd	12pm	Arrived	
"	24th	–	Superintended distribution of Remounts & inspected Brigade of Artillery	
"		8pm	Marched out	
NOEUX LES MINES	25th	4am	Arrived.	
"	"	11am	Marched out	
PHILOSOPHE	"	1pm	Arrived. Division went into action. Visited advanced Dressing Station. Interviewed the Vety Officers [illegible]	
"	29th	9pm	Marched out – Animals evacuated to MVS [illegible], and killed about 300, [illegible] Div H.Q. [illegible] at PHILOSOPHE.	

Army Form C. 2118

ADVS 21 Div

WAR DIARY
~~or~~
~~INTELLIGENCE SUMMARY~~
(Erase heading not required.)

Instructions regarding War Diaries and Intelligence Summaries are contained in F. S. Regs., Part II. and the Staff Manual respectively. Title Pages will be prepared in manuscript.

Place	Date	Hour	Summary of Events and Information	Remarks and references to Appendices
BETHUNE	Sept 29th	2 am	arrived.	
"	30th	3 pm	marched out. Reported that Sergt. Randall S. No 7503 4th 95th Bde R.F.A. was accidentally killed.	
LIETTRES	"	10 pm	arrived.	
"	Oct 1st	9 Am	marched out.	
MORBECQUE	"	2 pm	arrived. Inspected MVS + 2 Brigades Infantry Transport animals.	
"	2nd	9 Am	marched out	
HONDEGHEM	"	6 pm	arrived	
"	2nd–6th	–	Inspected MVS with DDVS 2nd Army, and all animals of the Division.	
"	6th	10.30 am	marched out.	
MERRIS	"	12.30 am	arrived.	
"	6th–31st	–	Inspection of animals of Division & general Routine. Very little sickness amongst animals of Division — a certain amount of Ringworm, which is being got under control.	

D Macdonald
~~Major AVC~~
ADVS 21 Div

1875 Wt. W593/826 1,000,000 4/15 J.B.C. & A. A.D.S.S./Forms/C. 2118.

121
7621

Q

H.Q. 21st Div:
A.D.V.S.

Vol: 2

Nov. 15

nil

Clm.

Instructions regarding War Diaries and Intelligence Summaries are contained in F. S. Regs., Part II. and the Staff Manual respectively. Title Pages will be prepared in manuscript.

WAR DIARY
or
INTELLIGENCE SUMMARY
(Erase heading not required.)

Army Form C. 2118

Place	Date	Hour	Summary of Events and Information	Remarks and references to Appendices
MERRIS	1/11/15	–	Arranging for erection of Horse Standings & Shelters at M.V.S.	
"	2/11/15	10 am	Interviewed DDVS 2nd Army. Gave instructions for Capt Chandler AVC to proceed to England to take up temporary commission.	
"	3/11/15	11 am	Inspected 95th Bde R.G.A. – Visited DDVS re Horse Float.	
"	4/11/15	10 am	Inspected Sth Irish Horse	
"	6/11/15		Visit from DDVS and visited M.V.S.	
"	7/11/15		Weekly return of Sick – 99 admitted – 94 cured – 13 transferred Sick – 4 Died – 1 destroyed. Shows outbreak of Ringworm checked.	
"	8/11/15	10 am	Inspected 380 mules being transferred from DAC to Indian Corps. Inspected DAC.	
"	10/11/15		Arranged with ADVS 50th Division about taking over premises & quarters & position for M.V.S. Rode out to inspect [illegible] [illegible] "East & South Divisions"	
"	11/11/15	9 am	M.V.S. moved to Nieppe	
"	12/11/15		Left Merris & arrived at ARMENTIERS. Headquarters at Ecole Professionnelle.	

D. Macdonald Major AVC
ADVS 2nd Div.

1875 Wt. W593/826 1,000,000 4/15 J.B.C. & A. A.D.S.S./Forms/C. 2118.

Army Form C. 2118

Instructions regarding War Diaries and Intelligence Summaries are contained in F. S. Regs., Part II. and the Staff Manual respectively. Title Pages will be prepared in manuscript.

WAR DIARY
or
INTELLIGENCE SUMMARY
(Erase heading not required.)

Place	Date	Hour	Summary of Events and Information	Remarks and references to Appendices
ARMENTIERES	13/11/15		Visited MVS at NIEPPE. also 62nd Infantry Brigade Transport	
"	14/11/15		weekly return / sick - admitted 125 - cured 71 - transferred sick 13 - died 3 - destroyed 2. Arranged for Veterinary attendance to 2 Mountain Battery.	
	15/11/15		Visited Remount Section to inspect Chargers for Head Quarter Staff and for one Brigade Commander.	
"	16/11/15		V.O. i/c 1st Canadian Heavy Battery reported at Office. V.O. i/c 50th Division Engineers reported.	
"	17/11/15		Met V.O. i/c 95th Bgde R.F.A. & inspected two Batteries	
	19/11/15		Visited DDVS at Hazebrouck	
	20/11/15		Inspected animals of 95th Bgde R.F.A. With C.R.E. inspecting Standings and Shelters. Weekly Return sick - admitted 186 - cured 116 - transferred sick 37 - died 3 - destroyed 8	
"	21/11/15		Inspected animals 62nd Infantry Brigade & 97th Brigade R.F.A.	

D Macdonald Major AVC
ADVS 21st Division

1875 Wt. W593/826 1,000,000 4/15 J.B.C. & A. A.D.S.S./Forms/C. 2118.

Instructions regarding War Diaries and Intelligence Summaries are contained in F. S. Regs., Part II. and the Staff Manual respectively. Title Pages will be prepared in manuscript.

WAR DIARY
or
INTELLIGENCE SUMMARY
(Erase heading not required.)

Army Form C. 2118

Place	Date	Hour	Summary of Events and Information	Remarks and references to Appendices
ARMENTIERS	23/11/15		Inspected animals 94th Brigade RFA – 63rd Infantry Brigade & 25th Mountain Battery.	
"	24/11/15		Inspected animals 96th ~~Infy~~ R.F.A. Brigade & 64th Infantry Brigade.	
"	25/11/15		Inspected animals of D.A.C.	
"	26/11/15		Inspected animals of Divisional Train. Weekly Return Sick – admitted 153 – Cured 97 – transferred sick 35 – Died 2 – Destroyed 1.	
"	27/11/15		Met DDVS at M.V.S.	
"	28/11/15		Arranged to meet DDR 2nd Army to inspect R.F.A. Bde Ammunition Columns.	
"	29/11/15		Visited M.V.S.	
	30/11/15		Made arrangements to inspect 1st Canadian Heavy Battery & 50th Divisional Engineers.	

D Macdonald Major AVC
ADVS 21st Division

1875 Wt. W593/826 1,000,000 4/15 J.B.C. & A. A.D.S.S./Forms/C. 2118.

Instructions regarding War Diaries and Intelligence Summaries are contained in F. S. Regs., Part II and the Staff Manual respectively. Title Pages will be prepared in manuscript.

WAR DIARY
or
INTELLIGENCE SUMMARY
(Erase heading not required.)

Army Form C. 2118

Place	Date	Hour	Summary of Events and Information	Remarks and references to Appendices
ARMENTIERES	1/12/15		Inspected animals of 1st Canadian Heavy Battery & 58th Div RE	
"	2/12/15		Visited MVS	
"	4/12/15		Accompanied Divisional Commander & DDR on tour of inspection of units.	
"	5/12/15		Inspected animals of No 2 Mountain Battery	
"	6/12/15		Arranging with VO 1/2nd Mountain Battery about Malleinisation of animals	
"	7/12/15		Visited MVS	
"	8/12/15		Inspected malleined animals of No 2 Mountain Battery & reported to DDVS	
"	9/12/15		Met Army Commander at his inspection of MVS.	
"	10/12/15		Inspected 95th Bgde Ammn Column	
"	13/12/15		Met DDVS 2nd Army about malleinisation of animals of the Division	
	14/12/15 to 30/12/15		– Carrying out Malleinisation of animals of Division. Daily inspection of different units	

D Macdonald
Major AVC
ADVS 21st Division

1875 Wt. W593/826 1,000,000 4/15 J.B.C. & A. A.D.S.S./Forms/C. 2118.

ADVS. 21st Div:
Vol: 4

Army Form C. 2118

Instructions regarding War Diaries and Intelligence Summaries are contained in F. S. Regs., Part II. and the Staff Manual respectively. Title Pages will be prepared in manuscript.

WAR DIARY
or
INTELLIGENCE SUMMARY
(Erase heading not required.)

Place	Date	Hour	Summary of Events and Information	Remarks and references to Appendices
ARMENTIÈRES	1/1/16		Despatches Mention Refer [illegible] DDVS –	
	5/1/16		Inspected animals 63 Inf Brigade	
	6/1/16		Inspected animals 95th Bde DAC RFA	
	7/1/16		Inspected animals 62nd Inf Brigade	
	8/1/16		Distribution of Remounts & inspection 94th RFA AC	
	10/1/16		Inspected 64th Inf Brigade Transport & visited MVS	
	11/1/16		Inspected [illegible] 126th Field Coy R.E. – Attended [illegible] ~~at~~ DAC.	
	12/1/16		Inspected 9[illegible]th R.F.A. Brigade & reported on condition of animals.	
	13/1/16		Visit from DDR and attended Casting of animals.	
	14/1/16		Visited MVS – Called on SSO & reported Shortage of Hay Ration.	
	15/1/16		OC MVS proceeds on leave – Visited MVS	
	18/1/16		Visited DAC & inspected animals	
	19/1/16		Inspected 200 animals of DAC (Working Party) at Steenwerck.	
	20/1/16		Inspected 65th Field Ambulance at Caestre & visited MVS	
	21/1/16		Distribution of Remounts	
	23/1/16		Inspected advance Section DAC animals & reported on same.	
	25/1/16		Proceeded on leave to England	

[illegible] Major AVC
ADVS [illegible] Division

1875 Wt. W593/826 1,000,000 4/15 J.B.C. & A. A.D.S.S./Forms/C. 2118.

A.D.H.S. 21st Div:
Vol. 5

WAR DIARY
or
~~INTELLIGENCE SUMMARY~~
(Erase heading not required.)

Army Form C. 2118

Place	Date	Hour	Summary of Events and Information	Remarks and references to Appendices
Armentières	4/2/16		Returned from leave	
"	6/2/16		Distribution of Remounts	
"	7/2/16		Inspected 94th Bgde RFA	
"	8/2/16		Visited DDVS.	
"	9/2/16		Inspected DAC and animals of M.M.G.	
"	10/2/16		Met DDR for inspection of DAC	
"	11/2/16		Visited MVS	
"	15/2/16		Wrote report on shortage of Hay Ration	
"	16/2/16		Visited Hospitals & Convalescent Horse Depot on L of C	
"	18/2/16		Met DDVS at MVS	
"	19/2/16		Inspected 97th Bde RFA	
"	20/2/16		Inspected Cast Horses of 1st Canadian HB	
"	21/2/16		Inspected 95th Bgde RFA	
"	24/2/16		Inspected 96th Bgde RFA	
"	25/2/16		Inspected 105th & 106th Field Coy RE	
"	28/2/16		Inspected Suspected Mange Cases at DAC	
"	29/2/16		Visited MVS & inspected Suspected Mange.	

A.D.V.S. 21st DIVISION Date

D Macdonald
Major AVC
ADVS 21st Division

1875 Wt. W593/826 1,000,000 4/15 J.B.C. & A. A.D.S.S./Forms/C. 2118.

ADVS

21st DW

Vol 6

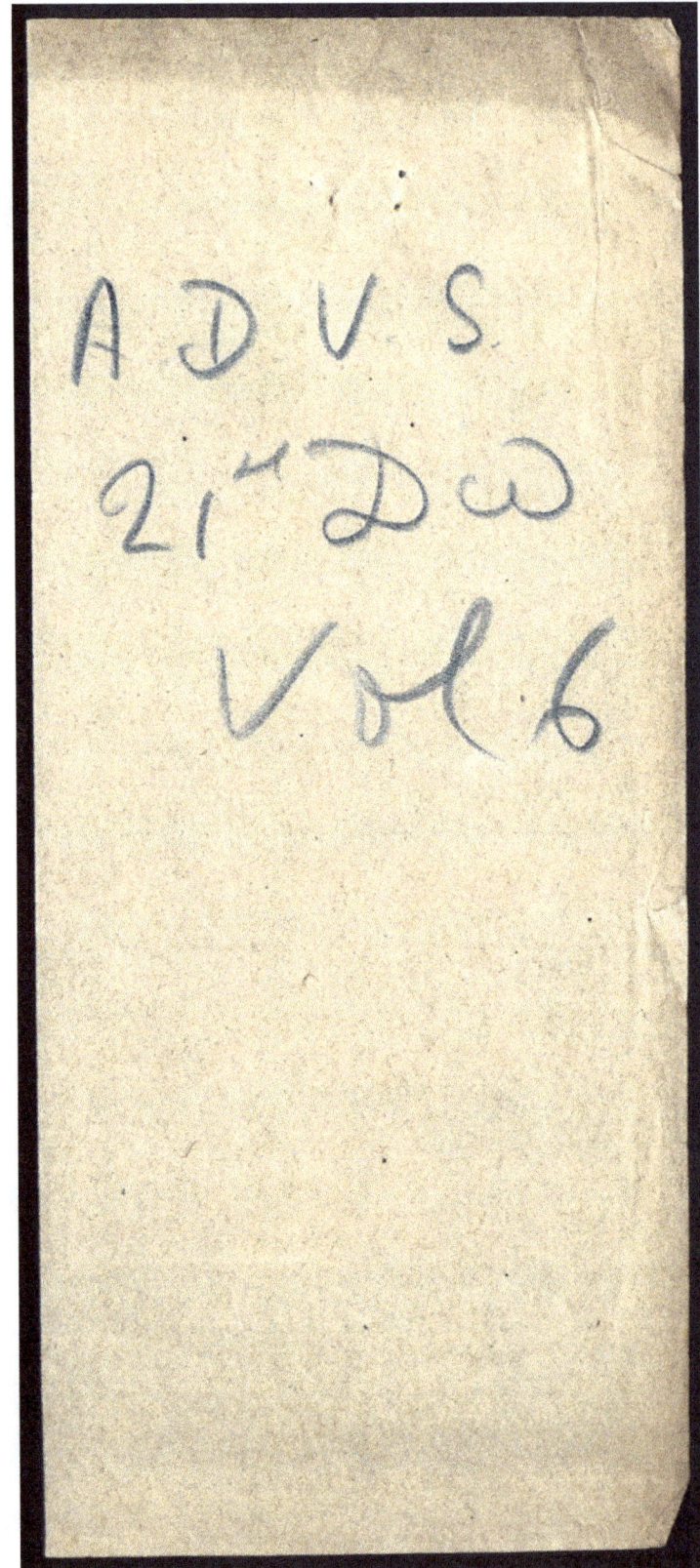

Instructions regarding War Diaries and Intelligence Summaries are contained in F. S. Regs., Part II. and the Staff Manual respectively. Title Pages will be prepared in manuscript.

WAR DIARY
or
INTELLIGENCE SUMMARY
(Erase heading not required.)

Army Form C. 2118

Place	Date	Hour	Summary of Events and Information	Remarks and references to Appendices
ARMENTIERES	1/3/16		Inspected 94th Bgde R.F.A. & report to A.Q.M.G.	
	2/3/16		Inspected M.V.S. & 126th F. Coy R.E.	
	3/3/16		Visited D.A.C.	
	7/3/16		Visited D.A.C. & reported to D.D.V.S.	
	10/3/16		Inspected Field Coys R.E.	
	15/3/16		Proceeded to MERRIS to select position for M.V.S.	
	19/3/16		Inspected Advanced Section D.A.C. & 94th Bgde Am Column	
	21/3/16		Inspected Remounts at distribution	
	23/3/16	10 a.m.	Left ARMENTIERES & arrived at MERRIS. [illegible] from D.D.V.S. there.	
	26/3/16		Inspected Several Units and interviewed Capt Sharpe A.V.C. at office	
	27/3/16		Capt Sharpe A.V.C. evacuated sick to Base.	
	29/3/16		Inspected 95th Bgde R.F.A. & inspected Remounts.	
	30/3/16	7 p.m.	Entrained H.Q. Animals at GODAERSVELT.	
	31/3/16	10 a.m.	Arrived at RIBEMONT.	

D Macdonald Major A.V.C.
A.D.V.S. 21st Division

1875 Wt. W593/826 1,000,000 4/15 J.B.C. & A. A.D.S.S./Forms/C. 2118.

A D V S
Army Form C. 2118
21 D W
Vol 7

WAR DIARY
or
~~INTELLIGENCE SUMMARY~~
(Erase heading not required.)

Instructions regarding War Diaries and Intelligence Summaries are contained in F. S. Regs., Part II. and the Staff Manual respectively. Title Pages will be prepared in manuscript.

Place	Date	Hour	Summary of Events and Information	Remarks and references to Appendices
Ribemont	1/4/16		Visited Corps. DDVS & DDR	
"	2/4/16		M.V.S arrived - Selected site	
"	3/4/16		Inspected 2 Section DAC	
"	4/4/16		Inspected MVS with DDVS	
"	8/4/16		Inspected 94th R.F.A. Brigade & 1 Section DAC	
"	9/4/16		Inspected 63rd Infantry Brigade Transport	
"	12/4/16		Inspected 2 Coy Divisional Train	
"	15/4/16		Inspected 95th R.F.A. Brigade & Ammunition Column	
"	16/4/16		Attended Distribution of Remounts with Staff Captain C.R.A.	
"	18/4/16		Inspected 4th Auxiliary Horse Transport	
"	20/4/16		Inspected 96th R.F.A. Brigade & 64th Infantry Brigade Transport	
"	21/4/16		Inspected one Batty 94th R.F.A. Brigade for Mange	
"	23/4/16		Inspected 97th R.F.A. Brigade	
"	25/4/16		Inspected 2 Coys Field/R.E.	
"	27/4/16		Selected advanced Dressing Station for MVS & inspected 62nd Infantry Brigade Transport	
"	28/4/16		Inspected Units at ~~[illegible]~~ Bonnay	
"	30/4/16		Visited one Batty 94th R.F.A. Brigade at ALBERT & M.V.S	

D Macdonald
Major AVC
ADVS 21st Division

1875 Wt. W593/826 1,000,000 4/15 J.B.C. & A. A.D.S.S./Forms/C. 2118.

Instructions regarding War Diaries and Intelligence Summaries are contained in F. S. Regs., Part II. and the Staff Manual respectively. Title Pages will be prepared in manuscript.

WAR DIARY
or
~~INTELLIGENCE SUMMARY~~
(Erase heading not required.)

Army Form C. 2118

A DVS
21st Div
Vol 8

Place	Date	Hour	Summary of Events and Information	Remarks and references to Appendices
Ribemont	1/5/16		Inspected MVS and RA wagon lines	
"	2/5/16		Visited MVS with Divisional Commander	
"	3/5/16		Inspected animals of 94th & 95th RFA Brigade	
"	5/5/16		Visited units at Daours.	
"	7/5/16		Attended Distribution of Remounts in the Division	
"	12/5/16		Inspected Infantry Brigade wagon lines	
"	13/5/16		Visited Hospitals line of Communication & School of Farriery Abbeville.	
"	16/5/16		Visited 15th Corps Heavy Artillery with Veterinary Officer	
"	20/5/16		Visited Advanced Section MVS & inspected wagon lines RFA	
"	21/5/16		Attended Distribution of Remounts with DAQMG	
"	22/5/16		Proceeded on leave to England	
"	31/5/16		Return from leave	

J Macdonald
Major AVC
ADVS 21st Division

1875 Wt. W593/826 1,000,000 4/15 J.B.C. & A. A.D.S.S./Forms/C. 2118.

Instructions regarding War Diaries and Intelligence Summaries are contained in F. S. Regs., Part II. and the Staff Manual respectively. Title Pages will be prepared in manuscript.

WAR DIARY
or
~~INTELLIGENCE SUMMARY~~
(Erase heading not required.)

Army Form C. 2118.

June

ADVS 21st DW

Vol 9

Place	Date	Hour	Summary of Events and Information	Remarks and references to Appendices
Ribemont	1/6/16		Visited Sections & Units	
"	2/6/16		Visited R.A. Wagon Lines	
"	4/6/16		Had Conference of Vet. Officers	
"	7/6/16		Attended distribution of Remounts & inspected DAC	
"	8/6/16		Inspected Wagon Lines in afternoon	
"	10/6/16		Inspected Evacuated Stables at Corbie	
"	11/6/16		Inspected Evacuated Mange Cases with Lieut. Turner AVC	
"	12/6/16		Visited additional Section & DAC	
"	14/6/16		Visited MVS & Wagon Lines Infantry Transport.	
"	18/6/16		Attended Conference at DDVS's Office	
"	19/6/16		Inspected Mange Cases at 63rd Field Ambulance Allonville	
"	22/6/16		Visited Infantry Brigade Transport.	
"	25/6/16		Attended distribution of Remounts	
"	26/6/16		Visited advanced Collecting Station & Wagon Lines	
"	28/6/16		Conference of VOs	
"	30/6/16		HQrs transferred to Ville. 5 Horses reported killed by Shell Fire.	

[illegible]
Major AVC
ADVS 21st Div

1875 Wt. W593/826 1,000,000 4/15 J.B.C. & A. A.D.S.S./Forms/C. 2118.

21 July

Army Form C. 2118

21 ADVS

WAR DIARY
or
~~INTELLIGENCE SUMMARY~~
(Erase heading not required.)

Instructions regarding War Diaries and Intelligence Summaries are contained in F. S. Regs., Part II. and the Staff Manual respectively. Title Pages will be prepared in manuscript.

Vol 10

Place	Date	Hour	Summary of Events and Information	Remarks and references to Appendices
VILLE	1/7/16	–	Inspected advanced Collecting station & saw VOs 95th 96th Bgde RFA re condition of horses & watering arrangements	
"	2/7/16	–	Visited MVS & attended distribution of Remounts.	
"	3/7/16	–	Inspected two Companies of Train. Saw VO i/c – Advanced Collecting Station withdrawn	
"	4/7/16	–	Proceeded to BELLOY-SUR-SOMME. Selected position for MVS	
Belloy-sur-Somme	5/7/16	–	Visited MVS at AILLY-SUR-SOMME & arranged for collection of horses left behind by other Divisions.	
"	6/7/16	–	Inspected 63rd Infantry Brigade Transport & 63 Field Ambulance	
"	7/7/16	–	Moved from ~~CAVILLON~~ BELLOY-SUR-SOMME to CAVILLON. Distributed Remounts.	
Ribemont	10/7/16	–	Moved from CAVILLON to RIBEMONT	
	12/7/16	–	Posted advanced Collecting Station at VIVIER MILL & inspected D.A.C.	
MEAULTE.	14/7/16	–	HQs transferred to MEAULTE. Inspected advanced Collecting Station & 94th RFA Bgde	
	18/7/16	–	Inspected MVS & attended distribution of Remounts. Inspected animals HQ Coy Train.	
	20/7/16	–	Office moved from MEAULTE to CAVILLON. Arranged for Vet attendance Infantry Bgdes etc	
Le Cauroy	22/7/16	–	Moved from CAVILLON to 3rd Army Area – Office at LE CAUROY.	
"	24/7/16	–	Inspected all attached Units & called to see DDVS 3rd Army	
"	26/7/16	–	Inspected animals Field Remount Section & 1st Indian Cavalry Remount Park.	
"	29/7/16	–	Visited HQs Artillery on line of march & saw the VOs regarding disposal of sick animals	
Duisans	30/7/16		Moved to DUISANS. MVS posted at HABARCQ.	
"	31/7/16		Visited 5th Sanitary Batt. at LOUEZ regarding animals unable to travel & inspected MVS in new position.	

D Macdonald Major AVC
ADVS 21st Division

1875 Wt. W593/826 1,000,000 4/15 J.B.C. & A. A.D.S.S./Forms/C. 2118.

Instructions regarding War Diaries and Intelligence Summaries are contained in F. S. Regs., Part II, and the Staff Manual respectively. Title Pages will be prepared in manuscript.

WAR DIARY
or
~~INTELLIGENCE~~ SUMMARY

(Erase heading not required).

Army Form C. 2118.

Vol 11

A D V S.

Place	Date	Hour	Summary of Events and Information	Remarks and references to Appendices
DUISANS	1/8/16		Inspected 62nd Infantry Brigade	
"	2/8/16		Inspected Field Artillery on line of march	
"	4/8/16		Conference with V.Os	
"	5/8/16		Inspected all standings & Overhead Horse Coverings in Div area with CRE VI Corps	
"	6/8/16		Attended distribution of Remounts at "AUBIGNY" Station	
"	8/8/16		Inspected Divisional first line transport with S.D.C	
"	11/8/16		Inspected 94th R.F.A Brigade	
"	13/8/16		Inspected 95th R.F.A Brigades & sent report to DDVS & CRA	
			Moved MVS from HABARCQ to AGNEZ.	
"	16/8/16		Inspected 96th R.F.A Brigade	
"	17/8/16		Inspected Field Ambulance Transport.	
"	18/8/16		Inspected MVS with DDVS 3rd Army	
"	19/8/16		OC MVS moved to SHQ for duty	
"	21/8/16		Attended distribution of Remounts at "AUBIGNY" Station	
"	23/8/16		Inspected 124th & 125th R.F.A Brigades attached to the Division	
"	24/8/16		Inspected 37th DAC	
"	25/8/16		Inspected 94th 95th & 96th R.F.A Brigades with DDVS 3rd Army.	
"	26/8/16		Conference of all V.Os	
"	28/8/16		Inspected first line transport of all Infantry Brigades with DDVS 3rd Army.	
"	29/8/16		Attended distribution of Remounts "AUBIGNY" Station	
"	31/8/16			

J Macdonald
Major AVC
ADVS 21st Div

BSD - B. M351/22/11. 12/15. 5000.

Instructions regarding War Diaries and Intelligence Summaries are contained in F. S. Regs., Part II, and the Staff Manual respectively. Title Pages will be prepared in manuscript.

WAR DIARY
or
~~INTELLIGENCE SUMMARY~~
(Erase heading not required).

Army Form C. 2118.

Vol 12

Place	Date	Hour	Summary of Events and Information	Remarks and references to Appendices
DUISANS	1/9/16		Visited animals of CRE & Divisional Headquarters	
	2/9/16		Inspected 124th Bde RFA & 37th DAC	
	4/9/16		Inspected animals of Divisional Train & interviewed OC MVS	
	5/9/16		Div HQs moved to LE CAUROY & MVS to same village	
LE CAUROY	6/9/16		Visited 63rd & 65th Field Ambulances	
	8/9/16		Inspected 97th Field Coy RE & MVS	
	10/9/16		Inspected 98th F Coy RE	
	12/9/16		Attended [illegible] of Remounts at Div Train	
	13/9/16		Div HQs moved to BUIRE Camp - Visited DDVS 4th Army	
	16/9/16		Inspected wagon lines DAC	
	17/9/16		Div HQs moved to FRICOURT. Visited 94th Bde RFA	
	19/9/16		Inspected 64th & 65th Field Ambulances	
	20/9/16		Visited Advanced Collecting Station at POMMIER Redoubt.	
	26/9/16		Inspected 91st Bde RFA.	
	27/9/16		Inspected 93rd Bde RFA & MVS	
	29/9/16		Inspected DAC wagon lines	
	30/9/16		Lieut WR Hunt [?] arrived to take over Vety charge of Div Train. Inspected Coys Div Train	

D Macdonald
Major AVC
ADVS 21st Div.

BSD - B. M351/22/11. 12/15. 5000.

Instructions regarding War Diaries and Intelligence Summaries are contained in F. S. Regs., Part II, and the Staff Manual respectively. Title Pages will be prepared in manuscript.

WAR DIARY
or
~~INTELLIGENCE SUMMARY~~

(Erase heading not required).

Army Form C. 2118.

ADVS 21 Div

Vol 13

Place	Date	Hour	Summary of Events and Information	Remarks and references to Appendices
Fricourt	1/10/16		Inspects MVS & 94th Bty RFA	
Buire	2/10/16		DAQ moved to BUIRE	
Ailly le Haut Clocher	3/10/16		moved to AILLY-LE-HAUT-CLOCHER	
"	5/10/16		MVS arrived FAMECHON.	
"	6/10/16		Attending distribution of Remounts	
"	7/10/16		moved from AILLY-LE-HAUT-CLOCHER	
Noeux les Mines	8/10/16		arrived NOEUX-LES-MINES. Visited by DDVS & DDR 1st Army	
	9/10/16		Inspects MVS Station NOEUX-LES-MINES.	
"	10/10/16		Inspected [illegible] Howitzer Batty 533rd	
"	11/10/16		Visited DDVS 1st Army & DDR.	
Sailly Labourse	12/10/16		moved to SAILLY-LABOURSE.	
	13/10/16		Visits ADVS 32nd Div & [illegible] [illegible] all Standings	
"	14/10/16		Took over [illegible] charge of MVS Billets in BETHUNE.	
"	16/10/16		Inspects [illegible] & [illegible] suspected case of Anthrax.	
"	18/10/16		Inspected 533rd H. Batty. [illegible] outbreak of Ringworm	
"	20/10/16		Inspects 62nd & 110th Infy Brigade Transport & Horse Bays at BETHUNE	
"	21/10/16		Met DDVS at BETHUNE re [illegible] & [illegible] & contemplated experiments.	
"	24/10/16		Attending distribution of Remounts	
"	26/10/16		Inspects 533rd How: Batty & 97, 98th & 126th Field Coy RE.	
"	27/10/16		Visits DDVS 1st Army with DR & DDR.	
"	28/10/16		Inspects Brigades of Artillery [illegible]	
"	29/10/16		Visits [illegible] re new VO [illegible] Transport with DDVS.	
"	30/10/16		Inspects Artillery Brigades & Infantry Brigade Transport	

[illegible] Macdonald [illegible]
ADVS

BSD - B. M351/22/11. 12/15. 5000.

NOVEMBER

WAR DIARY
or
~~INTELLIGENCE SUMMARY~~
(Erase heading not required.)

A.D.V.S. 21st DIVISION

Army Form C. 2118

Vol 14

Instructions regarding War Diaries and Intelligence Summaries are contained in F. S. Regs., Part II. and the Staff Manual respectively. Title Pages will be prepared in manuscript.

Place	Date	Hour	Summary of Events and Information	Remarks and references to Appendices
[illegible]	1/11/16		Inspected two Howitzer Batteries & 64th Infantry Brigade Transport.	
"	2/11/16		Inspected 90th Bgde RFA	
"	5/11/16		Attended Conference of ADVSs at Army Headquarters	
"	6/11/16		Attended distribution of Remounts	
"	7/11/16		Inspected No 1 Sect DAC & attended distribution of Remounts to Artillery Units.	
"	8/11/16		Inspected 110th Infantry Bgde Transport with VO.	
"	10/11/16		Inspected 96th RFA Wagon Lines with VO.	
"	11/11/16		Visited MVS	
	12/11/16		Inspected 63rd 64th & 65th Field Ambulance Wagon Trains	
	16/11/16		Inspected wagon lines of 94th Bgde RFA	
	17/11/16		Visited MVS & 65 Field Ambulance.	
	18/11/16		Inspected animals of Divisional Signal Coy	
	19/11/16		Inspected Divisional Train wagon lines	
	21/11/16		Visited MVS	
	22/11/16		Went on Leave to England	

[illegible]
Major AVC
ADVS 21st Div

1875 Wt. W593/826 1,000,000 4/15 J.B.C. & A. A.D.S.S./Forms/C. 2118.

"Q" BRANCH.
H.Q.,
21ST DIVISION.
No. A.1187.
Date

SECRET.

To:-
A.G's Office,
BASE.

Reference your C.R. 140/1503, dated 5.1.17.

Herewith War Diaries for November for the undermentioned. The Diary of the Signal Company was posted direct to you by that Unit.

33rd Mob.Vet.Sec.
A.D.V.S.

H.Q. 21st Div.
18.1.17.

[signature] Maj
Major-General,
Commanding 21st Division.

ADVS 21st Division Vol 15

Army Form C. 2118

Instructions regarding War Diaries and Intelligence Summaries are contained in F. S. Regs., Part II and the Staff Manual respectively. Title Pages will be prepared in manuscript.

WAR DIARY
or
~~INTELLIGENCE SUMMARY~~
(Erase heading not required.)

Place	Date	Hour	Summary of Events and Information	Remarks and references to Appendices
Sailly les Bourse	2/12/16		Returns from leave. Visits MVS	
"	4/12/16		Inspects 94th Bgde RFA	
"	6/12/16		Inspects Divisional Train	
"	8/12/16		Inspects 37 Coy RE	
"	9/12/16		Inspects 95th Bgde RFA	
"	11/12/16		Inspects 3 Batteries RFA with DDVS – Cases of suspected mange	
"	12/12/16		Attends distribution of Remounts	
"	13/12/16		Inspects Batteries 94th Bgde RFA & 95th Bgde – Suspected mange	
"	15/12/16		Inspects MVS & 2 Section DAC	
"	18/12/16		Inspects 95th Bgde RFA. Arranges for Lt Wallace AVC to take over charge 94th Bgde RFA	
"	20/12/16		Inspects Wagon Lines Infantry Transport at Sailly-les-Bourse & Noeux-les-Mines	
"	22/12/16		Inspects 3 Section DAC & visits MVS	
	23/12/16		Inspects 64th F. Ambulance	
	26/12/16		Visits Divisional Train & 2 Section DAC with VOS	
	28/12/16		Inspects Wagon Lines 95th & 96th Bgdes RFA	
	29/12/16		Office moved to LABEUVRIERE	
	30/12/16		Inspects 110th Infantry Bgde Transport	
	31/12/16		Visits MVS & arranges for transference to Bethune.	

[signature] Major AVC
ADVS 21st Div

1875 Wt. W593/826 1,000,000 4/15 J.B.C. & A. A.D.S.S./Forms/C. 2118.

"Q" BRANCH.
H.Q.,
21st DIVISION.
No. A/1187.
Date.

To:-

A.G.'s Office,

BASE.

Herewith War Diary for A.D.V.S., 21st Division for the month of January 1917.

K.H. Bruce Major

for Major-General,
Commanding 21st Division.

H.Q., 21st Div.,
11/3/17.

Instructions regarding War Diaries and Intelligence Summaries are contained in F. S. Regs., Part II. and the Staff Manual respectively. Title pages will be prepared in manuscript.

WAR DIARY
or
~~INTELLIGENCE SUMMARY.~~
(*Erase heading not required.*)

Army Form C. 2118.

ADVS
21st Division

Hour, Date, Place	Summary of Events and Information	Remarks and references to Appendices
LABEURIERE	1 - 28 - 1/17. Animals in wretched condition in back Area - Up to Knees and Hocks in mud - Fell away in condition, some almost to Skeletons. DDVS 1st Army inspected Artillery units 22/1/17 and sent in a very unfavourable report to the Division. Mange had broken out rather seriously owing principally to Clipping order not being carried out. Animals were certainly under rather unfavourable conditions, but I consider a lot more could be done in the way of providing nosebags & keeping them in proper repair, and the use of Hay nets does not seem to be Generally appreciated. Stable management generally in Artillery units in the Division is far	Vol 16 & 17

WAR DIARY
or
~~INTELLIGENCE SUMMARY.~~
(Erase heading not required.)

Army Form C. 2118.

Instructions regarding War Diaries and Intelligence Summaries are contained in F. S. Regs., Part II. and the Staff Manual respectively. Title pages will be prepared in manuscript.

Hour, Date, Place	Summary of Events and Information	Remarks and references to Appendices
	far satisfactory at front.	
28-1-17	HQs moved to WORMHOUDT.	
	One Battery at the last moment found it was immobile owing to Evacuation for "Mange", but fortunately was able to get some animals from a Brigade that was being split up, & managed to arrive at WATOU.	
	Watering arrangements on line of march practically nil — a few troughs here and there but majority of animals watered at ponds. 9 cases of "Stomatitis Pustulosa" were reported within 3 days of arrival by 94th Bde R.F.A. They were sent to M.V.S. & no further cases occurred. V.O. i/c took prompt &	

Instructions regarding War Diaries and Intelligence Summaries are contained in F. S. Regs., Part II. and the Staff Manual respectively. Title pages will be prepared in manuscript.

WAR DIARY
or
~~INTELLIGENCE SUMMARY.~~
(*Erase heading not required.*)

Army Form C. 2118.

ADVS
Feb. 1917

Place	Date	Hour	Summary of Events and Information	Remarks and references to Appendices
			Effective measures to prevent spread of the Disease.	
WORMHOUT	3/2/17		Inspected 95th Bde. R.F.A. – Found H.Qrs in bad condition. Several cases of debilitated and mangy animals	
			A 95 R.F.A. bad condition and 4 cases of mange.	
			B 95 R.F.A. Fairly good condition. Clipping very backward and 12 cases of mange.	
			C/95 R.F.A. Very poor condition – Bad stable management – 6 cases of mange.	
			D 95 R.F.A. Condition good, and no cases of skin disease	
			Bad mange cases sent to M.V.S. All slight cases & in-contacts dressed. Reported to D.D.V.S. 2nd Army condition of affairs & sent copy to A.Q.M.G.	
	5/2/17		Inspected 94th Bde. R.F.A.	
			A 94 R.F.A. Very poor condition – no Hay nets	
			B 94 R.F.A. Fair condition – 9 cases ~~suspicious~~ mange. no Hay nets.	

T2134. Wt. W708–776. 500000. 4/15. Sir J. C. & S.

Instructions regarding War Diaries and Intelligence Summaries are contained in F. S. Regs., Part II. and the Staff Manual respectively. Title pages will be prepared in manuscript.

WAR DIARY

or

~~INTELLIGENCE SUMMARY~~

(Erase heading not required.)

Army Form C. 2118.

Place	Date	Hour	Summary of Events and Information	Remarks and references to Appendices
WORMHOUT	5/2/17		C 94/RFA Poor condition. No Hay nets	
			D 94/RFA 6 Cases "Stomatitis Pustulosa" Condition fair. No Hay nets.	
			Reported to CRA about Haynets & sent copy to A P M G	
"	9/2/17		One Battery – B 94/– put through the Horse Dipping Bath at POPERINGHE, also H Q 95th Bgde R.F.A.	
	12/2/17		HQs moved to BETHUNE.	
	14/2/17		Inspected Ambulances & 110th Transport Lines. Stable management & condition of animals excellent.	
	16/2/17		HQs moved to SAILLY-LABOURSE.	
			All animals on standings & most under cover for first time since 28/12/16.	
			R Macdonald Major AVC ADVS 21st Div.	

T2134. Wt. W708—776. 500000. 4/15. Sir J. C. & S.

WAR DIARY
or
~~INTELLIGENCE SUMMARY.~~
(Erase heading not required.)

Army Form C. 2118.

ADVS
21st Division

Instructions regarding War Diaries and Intelligence Summaries are contained in F. S. Regs., Part II. and the Staff Manual respectively. Title pages will be prepared in manuscript.

Hour, Date, Place	Summary of Events and Information	Remarks and references to Appendices
SAILLY-LABOURSE		Vol 18
1/3/17. – 11/3/17	Animals on standings & under cover, but food quite inadequate to get them into proper condition for relatively hard work.	
LUCHEUX.		
" 12/3/17 – " 29/3/17.	94th Bde. R.F.A. inspected – majority of animals in very poor condition. Inspected [illegible] Bde Infantry & Pioneers. – All in good condition.	
BAVINCOURT. 29/3/17.	Watering arrangements good. Stable management in Artillery Units much improved, but animals are in very poor condition, owing principally to lack of food & weather conditions.	
	J Macdonald Major AVC ADVS 21st Div	

(9 29 6) W 2794 100,000 8/14 H W V Forms/C. 2118/11

Instructions regarding War Diaries and Intelligence Summaries are contained in F. S. Regs., Part II. and the Staff Manual respectively. Title pages will be prepared in manuscript.

WAR DIARY
or
~~INTELLIGENCE~~ SUMMARY.
(Erase heading not required.)

Vol 19

Army Form C. 2118.

A.D.V.S. 21st Division

Hour, Date, Place	Summary of Events and Information	Remarks and references to Appendices
BAVINCOURT 1-4-17 to 4-4-17	Advanced Dressing & Collecting Station opened at ADINFER. Weather conditions bad. Cold and wet. 70 debilitated Animals belonging to 21st & 58th Divisional Artillery were transferred to the Base. Animals working night and day under trying conditions. Rations quite inadequate.	
ADINFER. 5-4-17 to 12-4-17	MVS at ADINFER. Advanced collecting station at BOISLEUX-au-MONT. 58th & 21st Div Artillery Suffering heavily in Horses. Severe work - weather conditions & short rations the cause of wastage - For three days no Hay ration. 184 animals transferred for Debility. 142 died from Exhaustion due to Exposure, hard work and underfeeding. 28 animals had to be destroyed from same cause.	
13-4-17 to 20-4-17	13 animals transferred to Base for Debility. 36 died and 20 destroyed from Exhaustion	
21-4-17 to 26-4-17	50 animals transferred for Debility. 3 died & 4 destroyed from Exhaustion	
HAMELINCOURT. 27-4-17 to 31-4-17	MVS at BOISLEUX-au-MONT. Food ration increased. Weather conditions improved and animals picking up. A certain amount of Grazing.	

[illegible signature]
ADVS 21st Div.

(9 29 6) W2794 100,000 8/14 H W V Forms/C. 2118/11

Instructions regarding War Diaries and Intelligence Summaries are contained in F. S. Regs., Part II. and the Staff Manual respectively. Title pages will be prepared in manuscript.

WAR DIARY
~~or~~
~~INTELLIGENCE~~ SUMMARY.
(*Erase heading not required.*)

Army Form C. 2118.

ADVS 21st Division

Hour, Date, Place	Summary of Events and Information	Remarks and references to Appendices
		Vol 20
HAMELINCOURT 1-5-17.	8 animals killed by shell-fire 110th Infy Brigade.	
" 12-5-17.	Animals of Artillery units picking up – Condition – Good grazing & Rations sufficient	
ADINFER WOOD. 13-5-17	Nothing of importance to record – a few cases of mange were sent to the the base	
31-5-17.		

D Macdonald
Major A.V.C.
ADVS 21st Div

(9 29 6) W2794 100,000 8/14 H W V Forms/C. 2118/11

Instructions regarding War Diaries and Intelligence Summaries are contained in F. S. Regs., Part II. and the Staff Manual respectively. Title pages will be prepared in manuscript.

WAR DIARY
or
INTELLIGENCE SUMMARY.
(Erase heading not required.)

Vol 21

Army Form C. 2118.

D.A.D.V.S.
21st Division

Hour, Date, Place	Summary of Events and Information	Remarks and references to Appendices
HAMELINCOURT 1-6-17 to 20-6-17.	50C Division & ADVS inspected animals of 94th & 95th RFA Bgdes on 2/6/17 – Condition much improved – Good grazing & full ration. Casualties low – Mange showing signs of increase. Division on 20/6/17 relieved by 33rd Division – Leaving artillery meanwhile to ADIVARTER. MVS in Centre of Village.	
20-6-17 to 30-6-17.	Mange still prevalent in artillery units. On 26/6/17 ADVS Corps inspected 94th Bde RFA 27/6/17 inspected 95th Bgde RFA. Considering condition of animals good but Stable management not quite what it might be. Mange becoming serious – Steps being taken for its control. D Macdonell Major DADVS 21st Div	

Instructions regarding War Diaries and Intelligence Summaries are contained in F. S. Regs., Part II. and the Staff Manual respectively. Title pages will be prepared in manuscript.

WAR DIARY
or
INTELLIGENCE SUMMARY.
(Erase heading not required.)

DADVS
21st Division

Army Form C. 2118.

Hour, Date, Place	Summary of Events and Information	Remarks and references to Appendices
		Vol 22
MOYENVILLE 1-7-17	Moves Headquarters from to ADINFER.	
	During the month 300 cases of mange were treated of these 50 were evacuated to the Bases, and 60 cured and returned to Units.	
	A mange camp was opened at BOISLEUX-AU-MONT under supervision of a Veterinary Officer.	
	It was found to work well & the disease appears to be well under control.	
	There have been a large number of mild cases of Ophthalmia.	
	Cellulitis was not so prevalent this month.	
	All units in Division were inspected by ADVS Corps & he reported satisfactorily on the condition of the animals.	
	D Macdonell DADVS 21st Div	

(9 29 6) W 2794 100,000 8/14 H W V Forms/C. 2118/11

21

Instructions regarding War Diaries and Intelligence Summaries are contained in F. S. Regs., Part II. and the Staff Manual respectively. Title pages will be prepared in manuscript.

WAR DIARY or INTELLIGENCE SUMMARY.

(*Erase heading not required.*)

Army Form C. 2118.

DADVS 21st Div

Hour, Date, Place	Summary of Events and Information	Remarks and references to Appendices
Moyenville 1-8-17 to 27th-8-17	General condition of animals of Division Good — Mange practically stamped out. Summer Horse management much improved	Vol 23
30-8-17	Mange Camp closed down — Animals receiving full Rations & doing well.	
DUISANS 27-8-17 to 31st-8-17	Inspected Infantry Regts — Pioneers & Field Coys R.E. also Field Ambulances — All in good condition & free from Skin Disease	
	D Macdonald Major AVC DADVS 21st Div	

21

Copy

Army Form C. 2118.

Instructions regarding War Diaries and Intelligence Summaries are contained in F. S. Regs., Part II. and the Staff Manual respectively. Title pages will be prepared in manuscript.

~~WAR DIARY~~
or
~~INTELLIGENCE SUMMARY.~~
(Erase heading not required.)

September 1917 DADVS 21st Division

Hour, Date, Place	Summary of Events and Information	Remarks and references to Appendices
		Vol 24
DUISANS. Sept. 1st - 16th.	Animals of Division doing well, Mange practically stamped out, with the exception of one Battery of Artillery, all the animals have improved in condition.	
CAESTRE. Sept. 16th - 23rd	Artillery moved to Second Army area, Visited them on 18th and 25th. Animals in the open and no standings.	
METEREN. Sept. 23rd - 29th SCOTTISH WOOD Sept. 29th -	Very few casualties - Animals doing well.	
	D Macdonald Major A.V.C. D.A.D.V.S. 21st Division.	

(9 29 6) W2794 100,000 8/14 H W V Forms/C. 2118/11

Instructions regarding War Diaries and Intelligence Summaries are contained in F. S. Regs., Part II. and the Staff Manual respectively. Title pages will be prepared in manuscript.

WAR DIARY
or
INTELLIGENCE SUMMARY.
(Erase heading not required.)

Army Form C. 2118.

DADVS 21st Division

Hour, Date, Place	Summary of Events and Information	Remarks and references to Appendices
		Vol 25
1 Oct to 8 Oct SCOTTISH WOOD	Animals in good condition on the whole with exception of one Battery of artillery - 30 mange - A good number of casualties from Shellfire Bombs.	
8th to 20th BLARINGHEM	Casualties for the month so far amount 329 - 110 destroyed	
20th to 23rd ZEVECOTEN		
23rd to 31st Oct CHATEAU SEGARD	On 26th Oct Clipping Depot was formed at MICMAC Camp.	
	D Macdonald Major MC DADVS 21st Div	

(9 29 6) W2794 100,000 8/14 H W V Forms/C. 2118/11

Instructions regarding War Diaries and Intelligence Summaries are contained in F. S. Regs., Part II. and the Staff Manual respectively. Title pages will be prepared in manuscript.

WAR DIARY
or
INTELLIGENCE SUMMARY.
(Erase heading not required.)

D.A.D.V.S
21st Division

Army Form C. 2118.

Hour, Date, Place	Summary of Events and Information	Remarks and references to Appendices
		Vol 26
CHATEAU SEGARD 1-11-17 to 16-11-17	Condition of animals in the Division generally good — Clipping Depot at Micmac Camp clipping out average of 100 animals a day Evacuations from MVS very heavy — due principally to Bombs	
VIEUX BERQUIN 16-11-17 BARLIN 18-11-17 VICTORY Camp 22-11-17	ADVS XIII Corps inspecting all units of the Division & considered animals in good condition with exception of Nos 1 & 2 Section DAC which he considered a bit light but not in bad condition. 5 Cases of mange were detected in	
VILLERS CHATEL	No 2 Section DAC & Evacuated	

D Macdonald
Captain
DADVS
21st Div

(9 29 6) W2794 100,000 8/14 H W V Forms/C. 2118/11

Instructions regarding War Diaries and Intelligence Summaries are contained in F. S. Regs., Part II. and the Staff Manual respectively. Title pages will be prepared in manuscript.

WAR DIARY
or
INTELLIGENCE SUMMARY.
(Erase heading not required.)

Army Form C. 2118.

Dec 1917 DADVS 21st Division

Hour, Date, Place	Summary of Events and Information	Remarks and references to Appendices
		9R 27
TINCOURT 1-12-17 to 24-12-17	Inspected all animals of the Division - All in fine condition and very little disease with the exception of Opthalmia which has been rather prevalent. About 10 of the worst cases were evacuated & the remainder treated in their own lines and worked. There are still a few cases occurring but not any serious ones. Mange is cropping up again - a case here and there in different units but nothing serious.	
	[illegible signature] Major DADVS 21st Div	
LONGAVESNES 24-12-17 to 31-12-17	Nothing to note	

(9 29 6) W2794 100,000 8/14 H W V Forms/C. 2118/11

Army Form C. 2118.

Instructions regarding War Diaries and Intelligence Summaries are contained in F. S. Regs., Part II. and the Staff Manual respectively. Title pages will be prepared in manuscript.

WAR DIARY
or
~~INTELLIGENCE SUMMARY.~~
(Erase heading not required.)

January 1918 DADVS 21st Division

Vol 28

Hour, Date, Place	Summary of Events and Information	Remarks and references to Appendices
LONGAVESNES 1-1-18 to 31-1-18	General condition and health of animals of the Division good. There was one outbreak of mange in No 2 Section DAC. 50 animals had to be evacuated. Remainder were dipped at intervals and the outbreak was checked. Ophthalmia appears to be on the increase. The worst cases are evacuated and slight cases treated in isolation. [illegible] regularly to treatment with Lugol's Solution. D Macdonald Major AVC DADVS 21st Div.	

(9 29 6) W2794 100,000 8/14 H W V Forms/C. 2118/11

||

Instructions regarding War Diaries and Intelligence Summaries are contained in F. S. Regs., Part II. and the Staff Manual respectively. Title pages will be prepared in manuscript.

February 1918

WAR DIARY
or
INTELLIGENCE SUMMARY.
(Erase heading not required.)

DADVS 21st Division

Army Form C. 2118.

Hour, Date, Place	Summary of Events and Information	Remarks and References to Appendices
1-2-18 LONGAVESNES	—	Vol 29
2-2-18	Div. HQ moved to HAUT-ALLAINES	
3-2-18 HAUT ALLAINES	Inspected Div Train - Animals in good condition - Few suspicious mange cases	
4-2-18 to 28-2-18 "	Inspected Transport 3/4 Queens - 94th & 95th RFA Bgds 2nd Lincolns, MMP animals - RE Coys. DAC 64th Field Ambulance. 62nd Infantry Brigade 64th Infantry Brigade, Divisional Machine Gun Battn. All animals in good condition & practically free from diseases with exception of a few mange cases.	
	[signature] Major AVC DADVS 21st Div —	

7

Instructions regarding War Diaries and Intelligence Summaries are contained in F. S. Regs., Part II. and the Staff Manual respectively. Title pages will be prepared in manuscript.

WAR DIARY
or
INTELLIGENCE SUMMARY.
(Erase heading not required.)

DADVS 21 D

Army Form C. 2118.

Vol 30

Place	Date	Hour	Summary of Events and Information	Remarks and references to Appendices
LONGAVESNES	1/3/18		Division moved to ~~HAUT ALLAINES~~ LONGAVESNES.	
	2/3/18		Conference at VII Corps.	
	3/3/18		Inspected 110th Infantry Bgde – Animals in good condition.	
	4/3/18		Inspected 62nd Infantry Bgde – Animals in good condition – moved MVS [illegible]	
	5/3/18		Inspected 64th " " " " " "	
	13/3/18		Proceeded on leave to England handing over to Capt [illegible] of 33rd MVS	
	21/3/18		Opening day of German Offensive – Capt W Hay AVC wounded. DADVS recalled from leave.	
TEMPLEUX LA FOSSE	22/3/18	12 noon	Div HQs moved & 24 hours later were [illegible] on to HAUT ALLAINES.	
	23/3/18		Div HQs moved to CLERY – stayed here 3 hours and then retreated to MARICOURT. DADVS rejoins Division.	
	24/3/18		Div HQs moved to BRAY.	
	25/3/18		" " " SAILLY LAURETTE & then to BRESLE	
	27/3/18		" " " BAVELINCOURT. Lieut E S [illegible] reports having arrived in relief of Capt W. Hay wounded.	
	30/4/18		Div HQs moved to ALLONVILLE. Inspected Field Artillery Brigades – all animals in good condition & stood the work wonderfully well.	
			Casualties during the Retirement	
			Horses with [illegible] 196 – 128 killed – 30 destroyed – 32 evacuated, missing 6 wounded	
			Mules with [illegible] 105 – 93 killed – 6 destroyed – 6 evacuated	
			Total casualties with [illegible] thus 301	
			[illegible] Major AVC DADVS 21st Divn	

D. D. & L., London, E.C. (A8001) Wt. W1771/M2031 750,000 5/17 Sch. 52 Forms/C2118/14

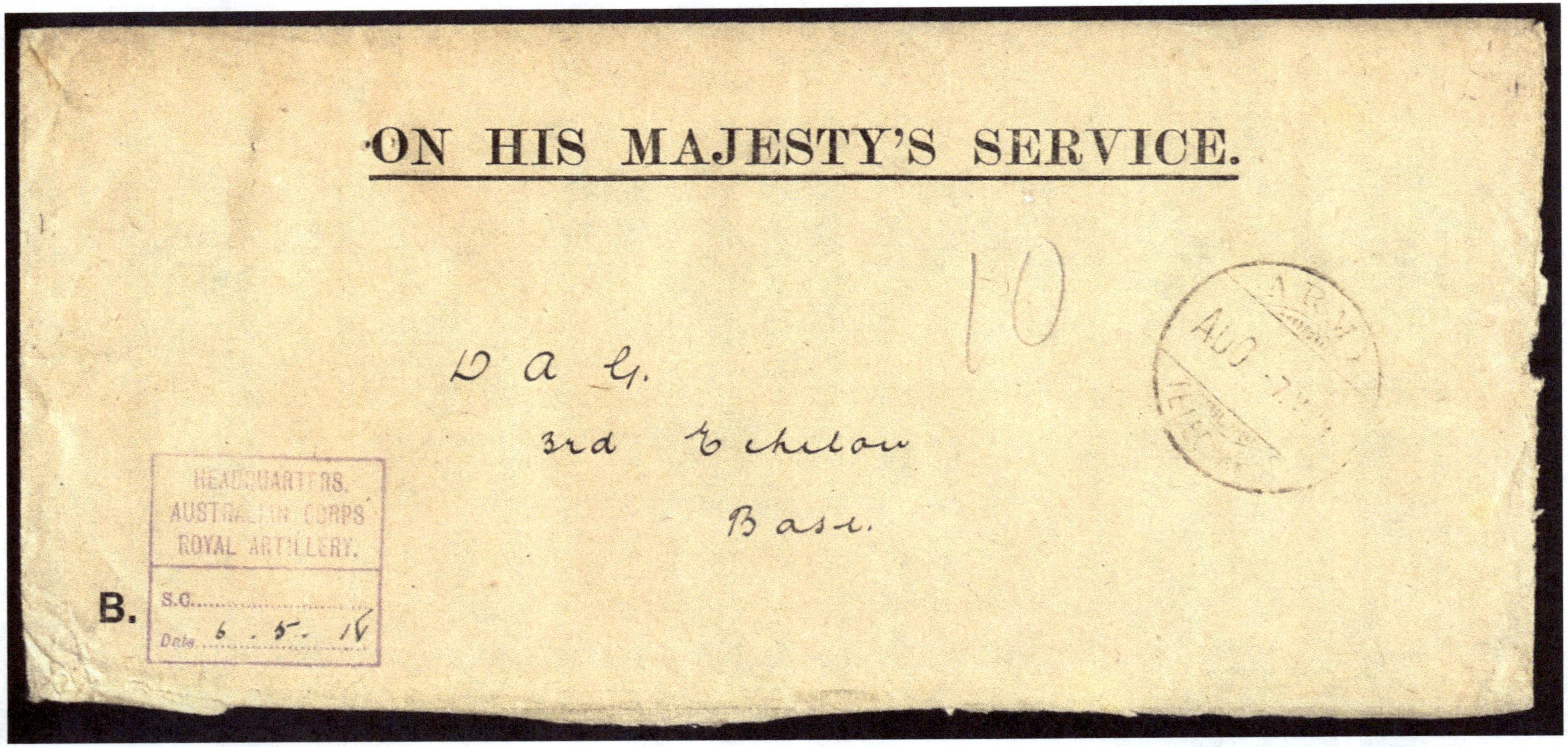
ON HIS MAJESTY'S SERVICE.
10
D A G.
3rd Echelon
Base.
ARMY
HEADQUARTERS.
AUSTRALIAN CORPS
ROYAL ARTILLERY.
S.C.
Date 6 . 5 . 16
B.

29 DADVS 21st Div.

WAR DIARY
or
INTELLIGENCE SUMMARY.
(*Erase heading not required.*)

Army Form C. 2118.

Instructions regarding War Diaries and Intelligence Summaries are contained in F. S. Regs., Part II. and the Staff Manual respectively. Title pages will be prepared in manuscript. April 1918

D.A.D.V.S. 21st DIVISION

Vol 31

Place	Date	Hour	Summary of Events and Information	Remarks and references to Appendices
DRANOUTRE	1-4-18 to 10-4-18		Inspected Infantry Transport - Field Ambulances and Divisional Train. Animals with exception of one Battn (1st East Yorks) in good condition and free from Skin disease	
CHATEAU-SEGARD	11-4-18		Inspected 3 Field Coys R.E. Animals in fair condition	
HOOGRAAF	17/4/18		118th Composite Bgde 39th Div came under my Veterinary administration	
POPERINGHE G16 a 5.2 Sheet 28	19-4-18 to 30/4/18		During this period Casualties from Gun Shot wounds were rather high — 14 Mules & 33 Horses in the Infantry. There were also 17 Cases of Gas poisoning. In most of these the Eyes were chiefly affected. It did not appear to me to be Mustard Gas, as there were no Skin lesions. Three had to be destroyed, the remainder were sent to the Base. Divisional Artillery were detached with the French during this period. I visited them on 22/4/18. They were getting a certain amount of grazing - were in fair condition & free from Skin disease. Casualties from all Causes slight	

B Macdonald Major AVC
DADVS 21st Div

6/

Instructions regarding War Diaries and Intelligence Summaries are contained in F. S. Regs., Part II. and the Staff Manual respectively. Title pages will be prepared in manuscript.

May 1918

WAR DIARY
or
~~INTELLIGENCE SUMMARY.~~
(Erase heading not required.)

Army Form C. 2118.

DADVS 21st Div

Vol 33

Place	Date	Hour	Summary of Events and Information	Remarks and references to Appendices
L 14.a.20	1-5-18		Division relieves 8th Div	
RUBROUCK	2-5-18		Division moves to this area less Artillery	
"	3-5-18		Div Artillery rejoins the Division	
	4-5-18		Div entraining at ST OMER	
ROMIGNY	5-5-18		Arrive in this area - Orders issued for all Stabling & Standings - Divisional area to be disinfected	
	8-5-18 to 15-5-18		Inspected Infantry Transport & all Artillery Units - Animals in good condition & free from skin disease.	
CHALONS LES-VERGEUR	"		Div relieves 71st French Division	
"	16-5-18 to 26-5-18		Inspected all units of the Division - with the exception of one Battn Infantry Transport they were all in good condition. This particular Battn had a number of Remounts up recently in rather poor condition. General condition of animals in the Division is very good.	
"	27-5-18	1 a.m.	Opening of German offensive. A great number of Gas Shells fell in Wagon Lines but the Animals did not appear to be much affected. No Mustard Gas. Sgt Smith W.O. D/94 Bde wounded during duty and evacuated.	
PROUILLY	28-5-18		Div HQ moves to this area & proceeded later to ROSNAY and then to SARCY when the ... the night. Next day Div HQs moved to LA NEUVILLE & following day to CHALTRAIT AUX BOIS less Artillery which remained in the Line.	
CHALTRAIT	31-5-18		Composite Infantry Bde formed & Capt Tinker AVC to proceed - Veterinary charge & Sergt King AVC ordered to accompany him.	
			Casualties from Shellfire during period 27-5-18 to 31-5-18 Horses 96 Mules 91	

D Macdonald Maj
DADVS 21st Div.

D. D. & L., London, E.C. (A8004) Wt. W1771/M2031 750,000 5/17 Sch. 52 Forms/C2118/14

1

VR 33. Army Form C. 2118.

WAR DIARY
or
~~INTELLIGENCE SUMMARY.~~
(Erase heading not required.)

DADVS 21st Division

Instructions regarding War Diaries and Intelligence Summaries are contained in F. S. Regs., Part II. and the Staff Manual respectively. Title pages will be prepared in manuscript.

June 1918

Place	Date	Hour	Summary of Events and Information	Remarks and references to Appendices
CHALTRAIT.	1-6-18 to 9-6-18		Capt. Tucker AVC detailed to take over Vety charge of Composite Brigade. Some difficulty in evacuation of sick animals. Wire from ADVS IX Corps that arrangements are being made to evacuate through the French. Inspected 64th Infantry Bde & 65th F.A. Inspected whole of the Artillery. Animals in good condition & improving daily. Free from contagious diseases. Attended Conference at IX Corps.	
LA NOOE	10-6-18 to		Div HQ opened here. Artillery & Composite Brigade detached with the French Army. Inspected No 4 Coy Train & MVS	
DISEMONT	15-6-18 to 18-6-18		Div HQ opened here. Artillery & Composite Bde still with French Army. Inspected 110th Infantry Bde Transport. Animals in good condition. Visited No 14 Vety Hospital ABBEVILLE	
	19-6-18		Composite Infantry Bde rejoined Division	
GAMACHES	22-6-18 to 30-6-18		Div HQ opened here. ~~Inspected 94th Bde~~. Artillery rejoined Division. Inspected 94th Bde R.F.A. Animals fallen away in condition a bit.	

D Macdonald.
Major AVC
DADVS 21st Div.

D. D. & L., London, E.C. (A8004) Wt. W1771/M2-31 750,000 5/17 Sch. 52 Forms/C2118/14

19

Instructions regarding War Diaries and Intelligence Summaries are contained in F. S. Regs., Part II. and the Staff Manual respectively. Title pages will be prepared in manuscript.

WAR DIARY
or
~~INTELLIGENCE SUMMARY.~~
(Erase heading not required.)

July 1918

Army Form C. 2118.

Vol 34

Place	Date	Hour	Summary of Events and Information	Remarks and references to Appendices
~~1-7-18~~			Division less Artillery moved here today.	
BEAUQUESNE	1-7-18		Inspected 62nd Infy Bde & 63rd Field Ambulance. Animals in good condition	
	2-7-18		Inspected 110th Infy Bde. Animals in good condition	
	3-7-18		Inspected 21st Machine Gun Battn – 100 Remounts recently received in very poor condition. Reported matter to GOC & ADVS V Corps & suggested that they be exchanged for mules	
	8-7-18		Visited HQ RA & inspected 94th Bde RFA – animals in fair condition	
	10-7-18		Inspected Machine Gun Battn with GOC. He agreed about Horses being exchanged for mules & representation to being made by him to the Army.	
	12-7-18		Suspected stomatitis amongst animals of 3rd Bde RHA attached temporarily to Division	
	13-7-18		Mild outbreak of Contagious Stomatitis – 20 cases in all. Reported to Corps and necessary precautions taken.	
	15-7-18		Inspected 3 Field Coys RE, 64th Infy Bde & 64th Field Amb. with Horse Advisor to V Corps. With exception of 1 Batt. 64th Bde animals in good condition. 7 fresh cases stomatitis in E Batty RHA	
	17-7-18		Inspected 110th Infy Bde, 14th Trench mortars & No 3 Coy Train with Horse Advisor to V Corps. Animals in fair condition. No further cases Stomatitis.	
	20-7-18		3rd Bde RHA left Divisional Area	
	22-7-18		Inspected Machine Gun Batt. with DDR 3rd Army DDVS & GOC – 30 animals cast	
RAINCHEVAL	25-7-18		Div relieved 63rd Division. Artillery rejoined Division. Inspected 62nd Infy Bde Transport & 3 Field Coys RE with ADVS V Corps	
	30-7-18		Attended Conference V Corps.	
	31-7-18		Inspected Div Artillery with ADVS V Corps – One Battery & one Section DAC in poor condition – Remainder fair to good. Reported [illegible] to GOC RA & Corps.	

D. Macdonald
Major AVC
DADVS 21st Div

D. D. & L., London, E.C.
(A8004) Wt. W1771/M2031 750,000 5/17 Sch. 52 Forms/C2118/14

7

Instructions regarding War Diaries and Intelligence Summaries are contained in F. S. Regs., Part II. and the Staff Manual respectively. Title pages will be prepared in manuscript.

WAR DIARY
or
~~INTELLIGENCE SUMMARY.~~
(Erase heading not required.)

Army Form C. 2118.

DADVS [illegible]

VR 35

Place	Date	Hour	Summary of Events and Information	Remarks and references to Appendices
RANCAGVAL	1-8-18		Two Cases [illegible] poisoning in Mules reported from 63rd F. Ambulance.	
	3-8-18		Inspected [illegible] [illegible] Batt. & [illegible] [illegible] debilitated animals.	
	5-8-18		Isolated 1 Case Suspected Epizootic Lymph. belonging to 93rd Regt. [illegible] microscopically. Sent pus to Base	
	6-8-18		Handed over to Capt [illegible] AVC and proceeded on Short Leave to England.	
	12-8-18		DDVS 3rd Army inspected Divisional Artillery. With exception of 3 Batteries and 1 Section DAC the report was satisfactory.	
	14-8-18		Capt [illegible] AVC was placed on Sick List.	
	20-8-18		Capt [illegible] taken off Sick List & returned to duty.	
	21-8-18		3rd Army Offensive Commenced. One man in MVS wounded by Bomb & Evacuated.	
	22-8-18		Capt [illegible] inspected 64th Infantry Bgde with Horse Advisor to V Corps. I returned from leave.	
	25-8-18		Office moved to ACHEUX. MVS. moved to MAILLY-MAILLET.	
	27-8-18		Visited advanced Div. H.Qrs & 64th Regt. Transport.	
	[illegible]-8-18		Visited [illegible] [illegible] Batt. Transport & SCa Section DAC	
	30-8-18		Capt [illegible] AVC proceeded on leave & Capt [illegible] AVC took over charge of 33rd MVS.	
	31-8-18		Visited advanced H.Qrs & Transport Lines & MVS	

[illegible] Macdonell
Major AVC
DADVS [illegible] Div.

D. D. & L., London, E.C. (A8004) Wt. W1771/M2031 750,000 5/17 Sch. 52 Forms/C2118/14

29

Instructions regarding War Diaries and Intelligence Summaries are contained in F. S. Regs., Part II. and the Staff Manual respectively. Title pages will be prepared in manuscript.

WAR DIARY
or
INTELLIGENCE SUMMARY.
(Erase heading not required.)

Army Form C. 2118.

D.A.D.V.S. 21st DIVISION.

Sept 1918 DADVS 21st Division

98/36

Place	Date	Hour	Summary of Events and Information	Remarks and references to Appendices
MAILLY-MAILLET	1-9-18		MVS moved to GRANDCOURT.	
LE SARS	6-9-18		Moved to M 9 c 9.9.	
LES BOEUFS	9-9-18		Moved to T 9 a 8.3 57C. Inspected No 3 Coy Train & MVS	
" "	11-9-18		Inspected D.A.C. & 63rd Field Ambulance	
" "	16-9-18		Capt Symonds OC MVS returned from leave	
" "	17-9-18		Capt Tucker AVC proceeded on leave. MVS moved to LE MESNIL.	
" "	19-9-18		16 captured German Horses admitted to MVS – very debilitated. unfit for work. Evacuated to VES V Corps.	
" "	20-9-18		Inspected 54th F Coy RE – very poor condition of animals reported to V Corps. Recently arrived from England.	
" "	21-9-18		Inspected 64th Infantry Bde Transport. 9th KOYLI & 1st East Yorks Transport in good condition	
" "	23-9-18		ADVS inspected 54th F Coy RE & visited my office. Inspected 95th Bde R.F.A. – animals in fair condition.	
" "	24-9-18		Visited No 14 Vety Hospital ABBEVILLE	
" "	26-9-18		95th Bde R.F.A. & No 2 Section DAC detached from Divn temporarily. Vety arrangements made with VI Corps	
" "	27-9-18		Inspected 110th Infantry Brigade & MVS	
" "	28-9-18		Office moved to LE MESNIL. Attended conference V Corps.	
			Died & destroyed for the month due to Shell & Bomb Wounds :- Horses 34 Mules 33.	

J Macdonald
Major AVC
DADVS 21st Div

D. D. & L., London, E.C. (A8004) Wt. W1771/M231 750,000 5/17 Sch. 52 Forms/C2118/14

30

1

Vol 38

CONFIDENTIAL.

WAR DIARY

D.A D.V.S., 21st Division.

October 1st - 31st 1918.

Instructions regarding War Diaries and Intelligence Summaries are contained in F. S. Regs., Part II. and the Staff Manual respectively. Title pages will be prepared in manuscript.

WAR DIARY
or
INTELLIGENCE SUMMARY.
(Erase heading not required.)

Army Form C. 2118.

Place	Date	Hour	Summary of Events and Information	Remarks and references to Appendices
LE MESNIL	1/10/18		Inspected 94th Bgde RFA & Divisional Train. Animals in fair condition. D 94th Bgde in rather poor condition.	
EQUANCOURT	6/10/18		Rear HQ moved here. Capt Hodgkin AVC proceeded on leave. 95th Bgde RFA rejoins the Division	
	8/10/18		HQ moved to REVELON Farm	
REVELON FARM	9/10/18		Division less Artillery relieved by 17th Division	
BANTOUZELLE	10/10/18		Office moved here. MVS also moved here	
WARLINCOURT	11/10/18		Office and MVS moved here	
	12/10/18		Inspected Infantry Bgde Transport of Division. 64th Bgde in poor condition. Reported to the GOC ADVS V Corps notified	
	14/10/18		Inspected Machine Gun Battn. Animals improved in condition since last inspection	
	15/10/18		Inspected Remounts and Field Ambulances	
INCHY	22/10/18		HQ moved to INCHY. Capt Hodgkin AVC returns from leave. Inspected DAC Animals in fair condition	
NEUVILLY	25/10/18		HQ moved here. MVS to INCHY. Inspected Signal Coy & SAA Section. Animals good condition	
	27/10/18		MVS moved to NEUVILLY.	
	30/10/18		Inspected 90th Bgde RFA. Animals in good condition with the exception of one Battery	
	31/10/18		Inspected 62nd Bgde Transport. Animals looking well.	
			62 Horses died (shortage for the month) due to Shell wounds chiefly when up the Line 32 Mules	
			[signature] Major AVC DADVS 21st Div	

17

Vol 39

C O N F I D E N T I A L.

WAR DIARY

OF

D.A.D.V.S., 21st Division.

FROM:- 1st November 1918. TO:- 30th November 1918.

Army Form C. 2118.

WAR DIARY
or
INTELLIGENCE SUMMARY.
(Erase heading not required.)

Instructions regarding War Diaries and Intelligence Summaries are contained in F. S. Regs., Part II. and the Staff Manual respectively. Title pages will be prepared in manuscript.

Place	Date	Hour	Summary of Events and Information	Remarks and references to Appendices
NEUVILLY	1/11/18		Inspected 94th Bgd RFA & 64th Field Ambulance.	
	2/11/18		Attended distribution of Remounts	
Poix du Nord	4/11/18		Moved to Poix du Nord. Moved 33rd MVS to VENDEGIES.	
	6/11/18		Under orders from AQMG joined 33rd MVS. Division relieved by 17th Division	
BERLEMONT	11/11/18		Orders from General Staff 21st Div. Hostilities will cease at 10.30 am today. Orders received in [illegible]. Inspected 110th Infantry Brigade in the afternoon. Animals in good condition.	
	13/11/18		Inspected 64th Infantry Brigade & 2 Coys RE. Animals in satisfactory condition.	
	15/11/18		Capt [illegible] OC 33rd MVS proceeded to England on special leave.	
	18/11/18		ADVS inspected MVS. Everything satisfactory.	
	20/11/18		Inspected whole of the artillery at NEUVILLY. Animals in fair condition	
	24/11/18		Inspected 98th Field Coy RE.	
	30/11/18		Inspected 62nd Bgd. Animals in good condition	

D. Macdonell
Major AVC
DADVS 21st Div

19

VR 40

C O N F I D E N T I A L.

WAR DIARY

OF

D.A.D.V.S., 21st Division.

FROM:- 1st December 1918. TO:- 31st December 1918.

Instructions regarding War Diaries and Intelligence Summaries are contained in F. S. Regs., Part II. and the Staff Manual respectively. Title pages will be prepared in manuscript.

WAR DIARY
or
INTELLIGENCE SUMMARY.
(Erase heading not required.)

Army Form C. 2118.

Place	Date	Hour	Summary of Events and Information	Remarks and references to Appendices
AULNOYE	1/12/18 to 16/12/18		Inspected animals of all units in Division. They are in generally fair condition & free from disease.	
MOLLIENS VIDAME	17/12/18 to 29/12/18		On 28th Dec commenced classification of animals RA D	
AILLY-SUR-SOMME	29/12/18 to 31/12/18		Classifying animals R.A.	

D Macdonald
Major RAVC
DADVS 21st Div

D. D. & L., London, E.C. (A8004) Wt. W1771/M2-31 750,000 5/17 Sch. 52 Forms/C2118/14

19

V8241

C O N F I D E N T I A L.

W A R   D I A R Y.

OF

D.A.D.V.S., 21st Division.

FROM:- 1st January 1919. TO:- 31st January 1919.

A.D.V.S.
21st DIVISION

Instructions regarding War Diaries and Intelligence Summaries are contained in F. S. Regs., Part II. and the Staff Manual respectively. Title pages will be prepared in manuscript.

WAR DIARY
or
INTELLIGENCE SUMMARY.
(Erase heading not required.)

Army Form C. 2118.

JANUARY 1919

Place	Date	Hour	Summary of Events and Information	Remarks and references to Appendices
AILLY-SUR-SOMME	1/1/19 to 15/1/19		Daily classification of animals of the Division for demobilisation.	
	16/1/19		Commenced mallei[n]ing of X & Z animals in Division	
	20/1/19		Case of Sporogenic Lymphangitis detected in C/94th Bty. RFA.	
	27/1/19		Inspected X animals for shipment to England	
	28/1/19		Inspected 94th Bgde RFA	

J. Macdonell
Major RAVC
DADVS 21st Div.

D. D. & L., London, E.C.
(A8004) Wt. W1771/M2931 750,000 5/17 Sch. 52 Forms/C2118/14

19

C O N F I D E N T I A L

WAR DIARY

OF

D.A.D.V.S., 21st Division.

FROM:- 1st February 1919. TO:- 28th February 1919.

Instructions regarding War Diaries and Intelligence Summaries are contained in F. S. Regs., Part II. and the Staff Manual respectively. Title Pages will be prepared in manuscript.

WAR DIARY
or
INTELLIGENCE SUMMARY
(Erase heading not required.)

Army Form C. 2118.

Feb 1919

Place	Date	~~Hour~~	Summary of Events and Information	Remarks and references to Appendices
AILLY		3/2/19	Inspected 51 Z animals before despatch for sale.	[illegible]
		4/2/19	Inspected 96 Y animals before despatch for England.	
		6/2/19	Major. Macdonald put on sick list. Capt. Pinder R.A.V.C. carrying on for D.A.D.V.S.	[illegible]
SUR		10/2/19	143 Y animals & 56 Z animals inspected	
		13/2/19	56 Y animals left division and inspected	[illegible]
		16/2/19	80 Y horses left division all inspected	
SOMME		18/2/19	Capt. E.G. Turner. D.S.O. R.A.V.C. reports for duty vice Major. Macdonald.	[illegible]
		19/2/19	100 Z animals sold at Torse from 94th Bde. R.F.A.	
		20/2/19	84 Z ~~animals~~ horses and 55 Z mules left Division for sale. 100 horses from 94th Bde R.F.A sold at Hornoy.	[illegible]
		23/2/19	Major. Macdonald went on leave	[illegible]
		24/2/19	155 Z mules left Division for sale	
		27/2/19	21 Z. horses 78 Z mules ~~left~~ Division for sale.	

E.G. Turner
Major. R.A.V.C.
D.A.D.V.S. 21st Div.

1875 Wt. W593/826 1,000,000 4/15 J.B.C. & A. A.D.S.S./Forms/C. 2118.

25

MARCH 1919

Army Form C. 2118.

Instructions regarding War Diaries and Intelligence Summaries are contained in F. S. Regs., Part II. and the Staff Manual respectively. Title pages will be prepared in manuscript.

WAR DIARY
or
~~INTELLIGENCE SUMMARY.~~

(Erase heading not required.)

Vol 43

Place	Date	~~Hour~~ Date	Summary of Events and Information	Remarks and references to Appendices
AILLY SUR SOMME	1/3/19 to 29/3/19	1/3/19	50 Z horses + 26 Z Mules left Division for Boundon all inspected.	
		2/3/19	58 Z horses + 42 Z Mules left Division for Boundon all inspected	
		4/3/19	169 Z horses + 137 Z Mules left Division for Boundon all inspected	
		5/3/19	97 X horses 73 Z horses + 25 Z Mules left Division all inspected	
		6/3/19	93 Z horses + 48 Z Mules left Division all inspected.	
		9/3/19	33 Y horses 78 X horses + 77 X Mules left Division	
PICQUIGNY	29/3/19 to 31/3/19	11/3/19	33 X HD 90 LDH X + 10 X Mules left Division	
		13/3/19	18 X LDH left Division all inspected.	
		16/3/19	60 X horses + 40 X Mules left Division all inspected.	
		20/3/19	25 Z Mules left Division	
		21/3/19	51 X horses + 2 Y horses left Division all inspected.	
		23/3/19	20 X horses + 40 X Mules left Division all inspected	
		24/3/19	46 X Mules left Division all inspected.	
		27/3/19	4 X horses left Division all inspected. Lieut G C Lay RAVC Departed for No 6 Vet Hosp	
		28/3/19	152 X Mules left Division all inspected.	
		29/3/19	Office moved to PICQUIGNY. Capt J. Hodgins RAVC left for Duty with London Division	
		31/3/19	Capt Pindar RAVC left for Duty with Midland Division.	

[signature]

Major RAVC

DADVS 21' Division

D. D. & L., London, E.C.
(A8004) Wt. W1771/M2-31 750,000 5/17 Sch. 52 Forms/C2118/14

www.ingramcontent.com/pod-product-compliance
Lightning Source LLC
Chambersburg PA
CBHW081241170426
43191CB00034B/2003